STILL BREATHING

STILL BREATHING

Urban Centigrade®
751 East 161 Street, Apt. 7A
Bronx, NY 10456
www.urbancentigrade.com
Email: wamuhu.mwaura@urbancentigrade.com

Urban Centigrade® logo is proprietary and copyright protected.
Designed by Antony Kamau.

Front cover image: CC0 (PUBLIC DOMAIN).
Back cover image: Philip Pryke licensed under CC by 2.0 (Attribution), image inverted and cropped.
Lettering and interior design by Wamuhu Mwaura.
Author photograph provided by Joe Allen, Jr.

Ordering Information, quantity sales:

Special discounts are available on quantity purchases by individuals, small businesses, and localized retailers. For details, contact the publisher at the address above. Orders by U.S. trade bookstores and wholesalers, please contact publisher via e-mail above.

ISBN: 978-0-9903043-4-0

Printed in the United States of America

STILL BREATHING

POETIC WORKS BY

JOE ALLEN, JR.

EDITED BY WAMUHU MWAURA

URBAN CENTIGRADE®
NEW YORK

TABLE OF CONTENTS

ƒ

NEXT CHAPTER

suspense hangs in the air
the noose tightens its fingers
on the storyline
I struggle to continue
prying , I loosen the strangling digits
there's more to be revealed
carry on if you dare
carefully navigate a true path
for lies ended on the previous page
redemption starts on my next intent,
the tale progresses
there'll be a "happily ever after"
sometime before "the end"

MA, MA

I.

Throw me some ice cream money
Quarter as weight
Dollar plummets evadingly
Dexterity amazing, all-star catch
From green pastures to cement
Bounding chains of despair, I run
Excessive headache
From eager ingestion
But love for the provider
Flows through my veins
As chills from my cone
Warm my spirit
Because she's always there

I hurt my knee
Alcohol, betadine, iodine, bandages
Had to be Mother-made products
Doctors don't do it the same
Her hands like faucets
That pour TLC continuously
Into each dilemma
Dosage perfect
All can be cured
Because she's always there

Look at my report card
My need for assurance
Answered with lips and arms
Of encouragement
Your release of love and me
Pushed me towards the life
We both spoke of
Unreached
Not her fault
Because she's always there

II.

Throw me some crack money
Quarters hit me as the explanation
That there is no more
Dexterity lacking, speed essential
From green pastures to cement
Bounding chains of well-being, I run
Excessive heart rate
From eager ingestion
Love for the provider
Pumps quickly to my chest organ
As warmth from the drug
Chills my spirit, I return for more money
Because she's always there

I sliced myself for sympathy
Scorn in the finger

Pointing towards medicine cabinet
In reality pointing out
Her hands like signs
Of disgust and discomfort
Of my new presence
With thinking nowhere near perfect
Never can be cured
But she's still there

Look at my achievements
I have self-assurance
Answers came from within
Living right with encouragement
Your release of love and me
Pushed me towards life
I couldn't handle
Now I've learned from your love
And I'm still here
Because you've always been there

THE PACKAGE HAS BEEN DELIVERED

The loss of my cellphone,
caused a dampening of my spirit.
I knew the job I interviewed for was calling,
but, the ringing I could not hear it.
You see, I know I acquired employment
with the outfit I displayed.
See, I was dressed as sharp as the keenest knife,
and, before I left the house I prayed.

FEDEX promised my replacement phone
would arrive within the week.
I misplaced the stupid tracking number,
through my house I started to seek.
I called after I retrieved said number,
but the parcel could not be found.
I rerouted my call to the great operator,
bending my knees and hitting the ground.

With my callback number inoperable,
no blue white orange truck in sight,
I let my patience and faith take over
and closed my eyes real tight.
I asked for exactly what I wanted
and never gave it a second thought,
the proper steps I had taken,
the battle already being fought.

The next day, I awoke,
and ventured to the store,
I tripped and fell and busted my lip
on something in front of the door.
I started to curse but regained my senses
and instead gave praise,
the culprit that had knocked me down
was the box missing for six days.

In the haste to plug in the charger,
in the midst of all my glee,
a sound started searching for my ear,
heavenly ringing not programmed by me.
In a state of shock, I almost missed the call;
realizing my voicemail was not ready,
I hit the answer button haltingly,
and my breathing became unsteady,

as the voice on the other end of the line
explained the job was mine.
I called to thank Federal Express
but could get no one on the line;
they had an office very near the store
so I thought I'd stop by on my way.
Their office was closed and a sign in the window
said no deliveries on Sunday.

"Mmm, mmm, mmm," I said to myself,
divine intervention paved the way,

all my worrying was for naught,
His awesomeness saved the day.
I thought back on all that led up to this
and when everything had been considered,
I realized that once my knees hit the floor
the package had already been delivered.

Rating System

Do you find yourself bragging
about things you've not done?

When asked who's in charge of this
always saying I'm the one.

In every conversation
know what you're talking about,

don't have any concrete connections,
but swear that you have clout...

Do you find yourself lonely,
need company all the time?

Portraying whom you're not,
imitating a talkative mime.

Call yourself a chameleon
because you constantly change;

do you ever look in the mirror
and the reflection's looking strange?

You must come to reality,
find out who you truly are,

try practicing humility,
even though you're a self-made star.

Let someone else guide you,
your controlling has been barred.

Then, let someone else rate you,
your approval should be by God.

EXTENSION

The realization that my life
is not yet over
has become a constant focal point
of what lies ahead.

Anxiety over future happenings
brings about inquisitions
of why I'm not dead,
the expiration date on my contract

seems to have been extended.

On October 24th, 1998
my life was temporarily ended.
I untangled the knots
that caused this event

and tied them back up again,
because the thought of beginning anew
had me thinking maybe this should end.
The burden of the work

that needed to be done

was more laborious than working out.
Of course, the act of continuously failing

brought about self-doubt.
I'm not the type to ask for help

but I had to learn to kill my pride,
seek out just what was needed
and with new rules I will abide.
See I'm a bender of all laws written

I'll contort them but won't let them break,

and then I watch them change before me,
just for any other bender's sake.
The mirror was my worst enemy
but it turned into a great alliance,

turned my vision inside out
and eliminated my defiance.
The assistance I sought
was at the ready

and to myself I became true.

I also told the truth about others,
so when around me, just be you,
I falsified my history
by portraying who I was not,

I challenged my rigid, non-thinking ego
and put myself upon the spot.

What you see before you
is what refurbished is supposed to mean.

See, I was washed and rinsed and washed again

and I'm still not totally clean;
but, there's a shine about me
and I hope it's visual to you.
I'm building from the inside out

and I hope I'm breaking through.
There's a reason why I'm still here on earth,
though the purpose has not become clear;
but, I'm not short of seeking it out.

Through every passing year,

I help others as I help myself,
that's a hand that I must lend
to make the most of my life's extension
before it truly ends.

FOGGY MIRROR

I must've been tripping
when I asked people to not call me junior.
You see I know children who wished their fathers
had something to do with their names.
Didn't want to be a carbon copy of anything
playing of those games

my ego and originality wouldn't allow.

But, as I look upon our differences
a lot of things look the same.
See, I'm not backing down
from most things in life
and to him I pass that blame,
bravery was a trait I acquired from him.

I used to think, "This man is crazy,"

just like I used to think later in his life,
"yo this man is lazy."
Let me disprove both those points,
tackling them one at a time.
I realized through further observance,
he was not out of his mind,

he knew when to stand up for things

and when he backed down he did it with grace.
When it was time to put the hard work in,
he was there at the designated place,
he said what he meant and meant what he said,
might not have backed up every word,
but, usually, the way he stated it,

caused hesitance when it was heard.

I watched him rise early for work every day,
that is until he retired.
Now, I'm diligent on my promptness to work
with the fear of getting fired.
You've heard the saying, "TV junkie,"
and I laughed at this as I wrote,

because when the ambulance came to get him,

he wouldn't let go of the remote.
In my home I'm considered the same.
I need to know where the remote can be found,
not just in some idle place or under the bed
or just laying around.
You couldn't touch his newspaper before he read it,

that was a felony at best,

even if he wasn't touching it,
nobody reads it 'til he finished the rest.

Don't fold mine, don't open it before me,
read the horoscope, or check a score,
if it seems that important to you
carry your inquisitions to the store.

They say I look like him,

but that is something I couldn't see,
and now I know I'm an image of him
and he continues to live through me.

CONGLOMERATE

J.A.   I took something and made it mine
flattery from imitation
a heist of gems
hope diamond, diadem
flawless comparison
these treasures hijacked
for usage of self
I am worth more

Yet, a seamstress I become
patches, larger swathes
each intricately complicated
woven simply into
a compilation, a suite

a concerto produced
blended puree
fitted instruments
reversed from a synthesized cacophony
fluid, smooth
the mixture undetected

Vehicle: Sight & Sound
B.C.   Shaft of light, images abound
motion pictures flood a darkened room
conveying scenarios

where digital eye and audience eager
find each other

Character:

E.K.
A tapestry deemed fit
to drape blood and bone
the directionless roam a stage
there are no encores
successors never born
eternity's author writes
this joining of flesh and soul

J.B.
Thug living meets literature loving
that's color blind , but has rhythm
inside a vision that's silent
but paints the perfect picture of existence

Setting:

A.K.
Our earth intrudes in silent flight
severing Luna's gaze from Ra
night grows darker
harboring a contemptuous sanguine orb

A.S.
morning is always young
yet the eye ages,
the moon endures
although it enters darkness
writing my light
on the edge of blindness

Theme:

J.B.

The eclipse of a poetic mind
within a moving picture
idea jigsaw of seven lobes
coagulated
set before your eyes

W.D

word play contains puzzlement
yet the solution is just a play of words
brought forth by thought
documented

Story:

R.J.

Welcome to our territory
recognize a spirited atmosphere
differences have been put to death
physical is no more
bonding eternal
strength a reflection of togetherness
welcome aboard

I hope you enjoy the ride!

DREAMS

false stories that seem real
no physical being to touch,
but somehow I feel
the fear from the monster
the joy from victory
it feels as though there's somebody else
living inside of me

closing my eyes trying to trace
all the things that are good
attempting to reopen them
when escaping something in the hood
scared of the snakes that are present
that cause me to have nightmares
lying in a hammock on vacation
not having any cares

which way will it take me
each night it's something new
last night I hung with Oprah
tonight it may be you

I believe they're insightful
and facing them is a given
future tests in your life
you pass to keep livin'

UNSUSPECTED CONNECTION

I tripped into bible study
after a brief stint
nosily peeked through a door
into prayer circle I went.

Lesson plan dealing with life and death
of course, the choice was there
depending on beliefs of some
down below or in the air.

The spiritual called connection
the flesh will cause divide
surrendering your own free will
peer pressure to decide.

Skeptical of said teacher
he used to roam the hood
the meaning of false prophets
could this be any good?

Reflections of my character
see I was not always true
open-mindedness startled me to think
how can I question who?

I'm standing here reborn, my friends

and upon my conviction
wouldn't think a book titled *Jesus Calls*
would end up in religious fiction.

Real or fake, discernment prevails
so it's not what, but how it's heard
no matter how this call was answered
I was beckoned by the word.

SELF-JUSTIFICATION

feeling like I fumbled the ball in this case
but the score shows different
the possession arrow is in my favor
but my directives have been spent
called up all my reserves but the inactive list rules
championship rings adorn my fingers
but I can't seem to find the jewels
standing at midfield

not knowing which way to go
I know the play called was an option
but do I hand off or do I throw
indecisive about my playlist
as the clock continues to tick
even though it is only 2nd Down
I'm thinking about a free kick
this will free the other team
to take charge and continue the game

my defense is weary because of doubt
let them score there is no shame
on second thought I may be humble
but never one to sit idly by
very outspoken on some trivial bull
when it's trying to act shy
buckled down and broke the negative huddle

practice makes the next play a piece of cake

continue to use what got you here
and alleviate mistakes
as the ball was hiked positive thinking took over
and I surveyed all the routes
decided in a go for it all
and felt the receiver out
as I projected my decision
a completion was in sight
I closed my eyes and faith prevailed
had to use all my might

I threw procrastination out the window
and tossed hope in the right direction
stood and watched the certain outcome
and hi-fived my protection
chest bumped my new found confidence
and when my rings once again were bared
they had a shine I've never seen
and the jewels had reappeared
realized at that point
this was a trick of human mind
I have now regained my swagger
I was a champion all the time

Let's Complain, or Not

The train is late,
my toe hurts,
people don't understand me,
why don't they like me?
It's me against the world,
why does this always happen to me?

Where's the blessing,
the thankfulness,
the gratitude?
The blessing is in the ability to complain,
the opportunity to change things in your favor,
becoming a better you
is being able to change
your perspective on things.

See I stopped striving for perfection
and started striving for progression.
The act of improving on something every day.
The best defense against criticism
is giving the critic more to be envious of.

I'm not promoting evocation of envy,
but its green head pops up
in our business consistently.
If your higher power blesses you

with all you need then what's the problem?

Is it lack of faith of self-doubt?
All things are possible through Christ.
Look where you are right now,
is it where you're supposed to be
or do you think a mistake was made,
and if so on who's part?

Take personal responsibility for your present
and solutions to improve where you are
will reveal themselves.
If you complain about something
and don't have a clue how to fix it
then shut up.

Let's complain or not!
The lessons not learned
are trials and tribulations
continuously faced.
merry-go-round and round
I don't know about you
but I want to get off!

No Going Back, but Still Seeking

Playing catch up
Confused
Physically I muse
Mentally I run
Forward facing
Backward tracing
Looking for missing chapters
Within text of stone
Unalterable

Jogging memory
Rearward in motion
Backtracking for expectations
Still unreached
Knowing the re-starting line
Means optimism
As racers look ahead

Pre-sighting goals
Causes continuous thinking
Patterns
Like shifting gears
Grinding within change
I downshift
To see the humongous imagery
The big picture (sidebar)

Realizing this race
Even if in first place
Is never won

Even with the right direction
Its length eternal
Mile by Mile by Mile
You never catch up!

Future Wealth

Future Millionaire
Not the lonely kind
Expired rulers of the U.S.
My friends, top dogs
One inventor, I believe he was a rapper
L.L., Jay-Z, something like that
C-Note yeah, yeah that's his name
Our relationship's impersonal
But makes me rich (momentarily)

Future Scholar
Most likely to succeed
JHS awarded
Prophecy fulfilled
Street master degree attained
Graduate school attendance
Taken daily for life
Classes start
When I step out my door
Life expectancy my diploma
Makes me mentally rich

Future Relative
Builder of bridges burnt
Or in need of repair
Cut like an umbilical cord

Separated but still part of
A structure
Whose branches spread
Like sound waves
Carrying grandma's lore
And old-wives' tales
To virgin ears
Who like vacuum cleaners
Suck up brain fodder
An attic of remembrances
Dusty but well preserved over time
Makes me Family Rich

Future Angel
Yes, mistakes have been made
Seen through eyes that were
Unseeing
Alive in way of the living dead
Unknowingly participating
In a suicidal Kool-Aid party
Celebrating my soon to be passing
Hand-rolled cigars distributed
Laced with riflemen wearing
Powdery white uniforms
Hunting brain cells
They shoot to kill
Recovery, my Calvary
Consists of me and my best soldier
Or me as His best soldier

Marching toward all battles
Head on I charge
My back up relentless
You know I give praise
Where praise is due
And all other praises
Come from You
I'm spiritually rich
And that makes my future
Wealthy!

SHADOWS

I saw you, and then again I didn't.
You're not too good an agent,
you stick too close, easy to detect.
Maybe I'm misinformed,
braining you as a spy,
your culpability sucks big time.
By chance, if you're on my side
and literally you are figuratively.

I figure you as projection protection
so when it's my time to shine
bodyguard-like never far, *voila*,
but when I'm an extinguished star
wandering in the night alone,
I need you most.

But in your exodus from darkness,
and your adherences to light,
I perceive cowardliness.
Pitch black, your enemy,
minute illumination your friend,
but from darkness you come
and for that I must forgive you.

Evaluation

Who in this room can move mountains?
Let that linger for just a while.

When the realization that we all can hits,
there'll be a universal smile.

Applause is in order --
"You the woman!" "You the man!"

that has accepted the instruction given,
incorporated it into your life.

And in an attempt to give it back
have gained the knowledge of your true self!

Look at the shine,
the erectness of the spine,

no slouching aloud,
I recognize the proud.

No arrogance showing,
because confidence brings truth,

chronological age means nothing,
born again brings youth.

PAL JOEY

they say the motions of one's body
can often be revealing
habitual faces and demeanor
may not always be appealing

the stature of some people
can sometimes be misleading
aggressive ways within one's self
can be the result of said one's being

sometimes teachings taken seriously
can easily be embedded
in the character of the person taught
but not that easily shed

if you take the strengths and use them
only accessing outside parts
you sometimes downplay the strongest muscle
that touches other's hearts

menacing monster or gentle giant
I shouldn't have to ask
I should recognize just who you are
so please remove your mask

flex your spirit and not your body

when expressing what you feel
the outcome from this encounter
will be so much more real

a very menacing presence
can shake some to the core
but a controlled intellect in the spirit
will scare a whole lot more!

SAME PLACES / DIFFERENT TIMES

Caught up in the grips of my cockiness,
felt myself slipping again,
the progression of my recession
simmered in a pot of insanity.

Some things change like arithmetic,
others are constants like time,
my change for good is gradual,
complacency means destruction.

The comfort zone of dangerous living,
became as elevator urine in the projects,
it's just there,
accepting or not is the key.

An ugly ending argument, a suspension, and bullpen therapy,
did a Jackie Joyner-Kersee sprint through my daily,
then slowed to a jogging memory of what I've become
and where I presently sat.

The stink of *déjà vu*,
murderer, on top of assaulter, drug seller,
pedophile, homeless, user, neighborhood kingpin
pyramid of illegality whose height World Trade.

Bringing a cacophony of sights and smells

that challenges gag reflex,
out of the frying pan into the pressure cooker
the menacing sweet old lady in a robe convenes,

felony, $3000 bail.
Fell flat on my face,
heard Marvin singing "Mercy, mercy me,"
and he was far from Gay.

Upon release of tension and physical self,
God's lesson became clarity.
Slow down, regroup, relax, relate, release *etc.*,
the paved path you follow, doesn't lead here.

perseverance!
3 trials, all tribulations,
began with mental relapse,
I was slapped back into reality.

To remain disciplined as well as determined,
to follow spiritual direction,
or end up in the same places
at different times.

For information regarding featured readings and general author appearances, please visit our website.

www.urbancentigrade.com

Printed in Great Britain
by Amazon

40649637R00030